EMMANUEL JOSEPH

The Sustainable Stitch, How Fashion, Ecology, and Ethics Are Sewing Change

Copyright © 2025 by Emmanuel Joseph

All rights reserved. No part of this publication may be reproduced, stored or transmitted in any form or by any means, electronic, mechanical, photocopying, recording, scanning, or otherwise without written permission from the publisher. It is illegal to copy this book, post it to a website, or distribute it by any other means without permission.

First edition

This book was professionally typeset on Reedsy. Find out more at reedsy.com

Contents

1	Chapter 1: The Fabric of Society	1
2	Chapter 2: Threading Through History	3
3	Chapter 3: The Environmental Cost	5
4	Chapter 4: Ethical Fashion Revolution	7
5	Chapter 5: The Circular Economy	9
6	Chapter 6: Green Innovations	11
7	Chapter 7: The Power of Consumers	13
8	Chapter 8: Sustainable Style Icons	15
9	Chapter 9: Local and Artisanal Movements	17
10	Chapter 10: The Intersection of Fashion and Activism	19
11	Chapter 11: Greenwashing and Transparency	21
12	Chapter 12: The Role of Policy and Regulation	23
13	Chapter 13: Education and Awareness	25
14	Chapter 14: Future of Sustainable Fashion	27
15	Chapter 15: Case Studies in Sustainability	29
16	Chapter 16: The Impact of COVID-19	31
17	Chapter 17: Sewing Change Together	33

1

Chapter 1: The Fabric of Society

Fashion is more than just clothing; it's a reflection of cultural values, aspirations, and identities. Clothing has been used throughout history to signify status, power, and even rebellion. From the elaborate garments of ancient royalty to the casual streetwear of today, fashion serves as a canvas for self-expression and a mirror of societal norms. However, as our wardrobes have evolved, so too have the methods and materials used to create them, bringing about significant environmental and social challenges.

The textile industry is one of the largest polluters in the world. Cotton farming, for instance, requires vast amounts of water and often relies on harmful pesticides that degrade the soil and harm local ecosystems. Synthetic fibers, while cheaper and more versatile, contribute to the growing problem of plastic pollution. The chemicals used in dyeing and finishing processes can contaminate water sources, posing risks to both human health and the environment. As fashion consumers, we often overlook these hidden costs, focusing instead on the allure of the latest trends and styles.

In recent years, there has been a growing awareness of the need for sustainable practices within the fashion industry. Ethical fashion aims to address both environmental and social issues by promoting fair labor practices, reducing waste, and using eco-friendly materials. Brands like Patagonia and Stella McCartney have set new standards by prioritizing transparency and social responsibility. Consumers are increasingly demanding more from the brands they support, leading to a shift in industry practices and a renewed focus on sustainability.

Yet, the journey toward a sustainable fashion industry is fraught with challenges. While some companies are genuinely committed to change, others engage in greenwashing—marketing themselves as sustainable without making meaningful improvements. It is crucial for consumers to be informed and vigilant, supporting brands that demonstrate genuine efforts to reduce their environmental footprint and improve labor conditions. By understanding the complex relationship between fashion, ecology, and ethics, we can make more conscious choices and contribute to a more sustainable future.

2

Chapter 2: Threading Through History

The history of fashion is a rich tapestry woven with stories of innovation and exploitation. From the intricate handwoven fabrics of ancient civilizations to the mass-produced garments of the industrial revolution, fashion has always been a reflection of the times. The advent of mechanized production in the 18th and 19th centuries revolutionized the industry, making clothing more accessible but also introducing new ethical dilemmas. Factories employed large numbers of workers, often in poor conditions, to meet the growing demand for cheap, fashionable clothing.

The rise of fast fashion in the late 20th century brought these issues to the forefront. Brands like Zara, H&M, and Forever 21 capitalized on the desire for affordable, trendy clothing, producing new styles at an unprecedented pace. However, this rapid production cycle came at a cost. Workers in developing countries were subjected to long hours, low wages, and unsafe working conditions. The Rana Plaza collapse in 2013, which killed over 1,100 garment workers in Bangladesh, highlighted the dark side of the fashion industry and sparked a global conversation about ethical fashion.

Despite these challenges, there have been significant advancements in the push for more ethical practices. Organizations like Fair Trade and initiatives like the Fashion Revolution movement have advocated for better working conditions and transparency in the supply chain. Consumers, too, have become more conscious of the impact of their purchasing decisions, demanding more accountability from brands. The history of fashion is not just a story of exploitation, but also one of resilience and progress.

As we look to the future, it is essential to learn from the past. By understanding the historical context of the fashion industry, we can better appreciate the complexity of the issues at hand and work towards more sustainable and ethical solutions. The journey towards a more just and equitable fashion industry requires a collective effort, and each step forward brings us closer to that goal.

3

Chapter 3: The Environmental Cost

Fashion's allure often blinds consumers to the ecological footprint left in its wake. The environmental impacts of the fashion industry are vast and varied, affecting everything from water and air quality to biodiversity and climate change. The production of raw materials, such as cotton and polyester, requires significant amounts of water, energy, and chemicals. Cotton farming, for example, is notorious for its high water usage and reliance on pesticides, which can lead to soil degradation and water pollution.

Synthetic fibers, while less resource-intensive to produce, contribute to the growing problem of plastic pollution. Microplastics from synthetic fabrics, such as polyester, are released into the environment during washing and can eventually make their way into oceans, harming marine life. The dyeing and finishing processes used in garment production also pose significant environmental risks. Toxic chemicals used in these processes can contaminate water sources, affecting both human health and ecosystems.

Transportation and distribution further add to the industry's carbon footprint. The globalization of the fashion supply chain means that garments are often produced in one part of the world, assembled in another, and sold in yet another. This extensive transportation network relies heavily on fossil fuels, contributing to greenhouse gas emissions and climate change. Additionally, the waste generated by the fashion industry is staggering. From textile scraps during production to discarded clothing in landfills, the amount of waste produced is a significant environmental concern.

To mitigate these impacts, it is crucial for both brands and consumers to embrace more sustainable practices. This includes choosing eco-friendly materials, such as organic cotton and recycled fibers, reducing waste through circular economy principles, and supporting brands that prioritize sustainability. By making more informed and conscious choices, we can help reduce the environmental footprint of the fashion industry and move towards a more sustainable future.

4

Chapter 4: Ethical Fashion Revolution

The rise of ethical fashion has brought attention to the need for fair labor practices and sustainable materials. Ethical fashion aims to address both environmental and social issues, promoting transparency, fair wages, and safe working conditions for garment workers. Brands like Patagonia and Stella McCartney have set new standards in the industry by prioritizing sustainability and social responsibility, proving that it is possible to balance profit with ethical practices.

One of the key principles of ethical fashion is transparency. Consumers have a right to know where and how their clothing is made. Brands that prioritize transparency often provide detailed information about their supply chains, including the factories they work with, the materials they use, and their environmental and social impact. This level of openness helps build trust with consumers and encourages other brands to follow suit.

Fair labor practices are another crucial aspect of ethical fashion. This includes ensuring that workers are paid fair wages, work in safe conditions, and have access to benefits and protections. Organizations like Fair Trade and the Ethical Trading Initiative work to promote these standards and hold brands accountable. By supporting brands that prioritize fair labor practices, consumers can help improve the lives of garment workers around the world.

Sustainable materials are also a vital component of ethical fashion. This includes using organic, recycled, and biodegradable materials that have a lower environmental impact. Brands are increasingly experimenting with innovative materials, such as lab-grown leather and plant-based fabrics, that offer more sustainable alternatives to traditional textiles. By choosing sustainable materials, brands can reduce their environmental footprint and contribute to a more circular economy.

5

Chapter 5: The Circular Economy

In a world of finite resources, the concept of a circular economy offers a promising solution. Unlike the traditional linear model of production and consumption, which follows a "take-make-dispose" approach, a circular economy seeks to create a closed-loop system where products are designed for longevity, reuse, and recyclability. In the fashion industry, this means rethinking how garments are designed, produced, and disposed of to minimize waste and resource consumption.

One of the key principles of the circular economy is designing for longevity. This involves creating high-quality, durable garments that can withstand the test of time. Brands like Patagonia and Eileen Fisher have embraced this approach, offering repair services and encouraging customers to buy fewer, but better-quality items. By focusing on durability and timeless design, brands can reduce the frequency of purchases and the overall demand for new clothing.

Upcycling and recycling are also essential components of the circular economy. Upcycling involves repurposing old or discarded garments into new products, giving them a second life and reducing waste. Brands like Re/Done and Rothy's have built their business models around upcycling, creating unique, stylish pieces from pre-existing materials. Recycling, on the other hand, involves breaking down garments into their raw materials and using them to create new fabrics. Advances in recycling technologies are making it increasingly possible to recycle even complex textile blends, offering a more sustainable solution to textile waste.

Extended producer responsibility (EPR) is another important aspect of the circular economy. This concept holds brands accountable for the entire lifecycle of their products, from production to disposal. EPR programs may include take-back schemes, where customers can return old garments for recycling or upcycling, and initiatives to reduce packaging waste. By taking responsibility for the end-of-life of their products, brands can help close the loop and create a more sustainable fashion system.

6

Chapter 6: Green Innovations

Technological advancements are transforming the way we produce and consume fashion. From lab-grown leather to biodegradable fabrics, green innovations are paving the way for a more sustainable industry. These innovations are not only reducing the environmental impact of fashion but also offering exciting new possibilities for design and production.

One of the most promising green innovations is the development of lab-grown leather, also known as cultured or bio-fabricated leather. This material is created by growing animal cells in a lab, eliminating the need for traditional livestock farming, which has significant environmental and ethical concerns. Lab-grown leather offers the same durability and aesthetic qualities as traditional leather but with a much smaller ecological footprint.

Biodegradable fabrics are another significant advancement. Unlike traditional synthetic fibers, which can take hundreds of years to decompose, biodegradable fabrics break down naturally in the environment, reducing waste and pollution. Materials such as Tencel, made from sustainably sourced wood pulp, and Piñatex, derived from pineapple leaf fibers, are gaining popularity for their eco-friendly properties and unique textures.

Digital fashion is also emerging as a sustainable alternative to traditional garment production. By creating virtual garments that can be worn in digital spaces, such as social media and video games, designers can reduce the need for physical clothing and the associated environmental impacts. Digital fashion allows for endless creativity and personalization, offering a new way for consumers to express their style without contributing to waste and pollution.

7

Chapter 7: The Power of Consumers

Consumers hold immense power in shaping the future of fashion. By demanding transparency and accountability, they can push brands to adopt more sustainable practices. The choices that consumers make every day, from the brands they support to the way they care for their clothing, have a significant impact on the fashion industry's sustainability.

One way consumers can make a difference is by supporting brands that prioritize sustainability and ethical practices. This includes choosing brands that are transparent about their supply chains, use eco-friendly materials, and pay fair wages to their workers. By voting with their wallets, consumers can encourage more brands to adopt sustainable practices and create a demand for responsible fashion.

Another important aspect of sustainable consumption is mindful shopping. This involves buying fewer, higher-quality items that are designed to last. Fast fashion encourages a cycle of constant consumption and disposal, leading to significant waste and environmental impact. By choosing timeless, versatile pieces and taking good care of their clothing, consumers can reduce their overall consumption and extend the lifespan of their garments.

Consumer activism is also a powerful tool for driving change. Campaigns like Fashion Revolution, which advocates for greater transparency and accountability in the fashion industry, have mobilized consumers around the world to demand better practices from brands. By participating in these movements and using their voices to advocate for change, consumers can play a crucial role in creating a more sustainable and ethical fashion industry.

8

Chapter 8: Sustainable Style Icons

Influencers and celebrities play a significant role in popularizing sustainable fashion. From Emma Watson's eco-friendly red carpet looks to Stella McCartney's vegan collections, these style icons are inspiring a new generation of conscious consumers. By using their platforms to promote sustainable brands and practices, they are helping to shift public perception and drive demand for ethical fashion.

Emma Watson, known for her work as an actress and activist, has been a vocal advocate for sustainable fashion. She frequently wears eco-friendly designs on the red carpet and has collaborated with brands like People Tree to create sustainable clothing lines. Watson's commitment to ethical fashion has inspired many of her fans to make more conscious choices and support sustainable brands.

Stella McCartney is another influential figure in the sustainable fashion movement. As a designer, she has made a name for herself by refusing to use leather, fur, and other animal products in her collections. McCartney's brand is known for its innovative use of sustainable materials and ethical production practices, setting a high standard for other designers to follow.

Social media influencers also play a crucial role in promoting sustainable fashion. By sharing their favorite eco-friendly brands and showcasing how they incorporate sustainability into their style, influencers can reach a wide audience and inspire positive change. Many influencers collaborate with sustainable brands on campaigns and product launches, helping to amplify their message and drive sales.

9

Chapter 9: Local and Artisanal Movements

The resurgence of local and artisanal fashion movements offers a counterpoint to the mass-produced fast fashion industry. By supporting local artisans and small businesses, consumers can help preserve traditional crafts and promote sustainable practices. These movements celebrate the unique qualities and cultural heritage of handmade garments, offering an alternative to the homogenized styles of fast fashion.

Local fashion movements emphasize the importance of sourcing materials and production locally. This not only reduces the carbon footprint associated with transportation but also supports local economies and communities. Brands like Alabama Chanin and Ace & Jig focus on creating garments using locally sourced materials and traditional techniques, fostering a sense of connection between consumers and the people who make their clothes.

Artisanal fashion celebrates the craftsmanship and artistry of handmade garments. By supporting artisans and preserving traditional techniques, consumers can help keep these skills alive for future generations. Brands like Maison Cléo and Injiri work with artisans to create one-of-a-kind pieces that reflect the rich cultural heritage of their regions. These garments often have a timeless quality, making them cherished additions to any wardrobe.

The slow fashion movement, which advocates for a more thoughtful and sustainable approach to fashion, is closely aligned with local and artisanal movements. Slow fashion encourages consumers to buy fewer, higher-quality items and to appreciate the craftsmanship and care that goes into each garment. By choosing slow fashion, consumers can support a more sustainable and ethical fashion industry while enjoying unique, beautifully made clothing.

10

Chapter 10: The Intersection of Fashion and Activism

Fashion has long been a vehicle for social and political expression. From suffragette white to Black Lives Matter tees, clothing can make powerful statements. Designers and brands have the ability to use their platforms to advocate for social justice and environmental causes, leveraging the universal language of fashion to spark conversation and inspire change.

The suffragette movement of the early 20th century is a prime example of fashion as a tool for activism. Suffragettes used fashion to convey their message, choosing white dresses to symbolize purity and virtue. This simple yet powerful visual statement helped draw attention to their cause and unify supporters. Similarly, the civil rights movement of the 1960s saw activists using fashion to challenge racial stereotypes and assert their identity and dignity.

In more recent years, fashion activism has taken on new forms. The Black Lives Matter movement has used clothing as a means of protest and solidarity, with slogans and symbols emblazoned on T-shirts, hoodies, and face masks. Brands and designers have also joined the movement, creating collections and campaigns that raise awareness and funds for social justice causes. Fashion's ability to capture attention and convey powerful messages makes it an effective tool for activism.

Environmental activism has also found a home in the fashion world. Brands like Patagonia and The North Face have used their platforms to advocate for climate action, promoting sustainable practices and supporting environmental organizations. By aligning their business practices with their values, these brands demonstrate that fashion can be a force for positive change. Consumers can support these efforts by choosing brands that prioritize sustainability and activism.

11

Chapter 11: Greenwashing and Transparency

As sustainability becomes a buzzword, some brands engage in greenwashing—misleading consumers about their environmental practices. Greenwashing can take many forms, from vague claims of eco-friendliness to deceptive marketing tactics that exaggerate a brand's commitment to sustainability. It is crucial for consumers to be able to identify greenwashing and seek out genuinely sustainable brands.

One common form of greenwashing is the use of ambiguous language and imagery. Brands may use terms like "natural," "eco-friendly," or "green" without providing specific details about their practices. They may also use images of nature, such as leaves or waterfalls, to create an impression of environmental responsibility. However, without concrete evidence and transparency, these claims can be misleading.

Transparency is key to building trust with consumers. Brands that are genuinely committed to sustainability often provide detailed information about their supply chains, materials, and practices. This includes publishing sustainability reports, sharing data on their environmental impact, and being open about their challenges and progress. Certifications and standards, such as Fair Trade and Global Organic Textile Standard (GOTS), can also help verify a brand's sustainability claims.

Consumers can play a role in combating greenwashing by demanding greater transparency and holding brands accountable. This includes asking questions, doing research, and supporting brands that provide clear and verifiable information about their sustainability efforts. By being informed and vigilant, consumers can help drive the fashion industry towards more genuine and impactful sustainability practices.

12

Chapter 12: The Role of Policy and Regulation

Government policies and regulations play a crucial role in shaping the fashion industry's sustainability efforts. From carbon taxes to garment worker protections, policy measures can drive significant improvements. Policymakers have the power to enforce standards, incentivize sustainable practices, and hold brands accountable for their environmental and social impact.

One important area of policy is environmental regulation. Governments can implement measures to reduce the fashion industry's ecological footprint, such as setting limits on water and energy usage, regulating chemical emissions, and promoting the use of sustainable materials. Carbon taxes and cap-and-trade systems can also incentivize brands to reduce their greenhouse gas emissions and invest in renewable energy.

Labor rights and protections are another critical aspect of fashion-related policy. Ensuring fair wages, safe working conditions, and labor rights for garment workers is essential for creating a more ethical fashion industry. Governments can enforce labor standards, monitor factory conditions, and support initiatives that promote fair trade and workers' rights. International cooperation and agreements can also help address labor issues in the global supply chain.

Policy measures can also encourage innovation and investment in sustainable practices. This includes providing funding and support for research and development of eco-friendly materials and technologies, as well as offering incentives for brands that adopt circular economy principles. By creating an enabling environment for sustainability, policymakers can help drive the transition to a more sustainable and ethical fashion industry.

13

Chapter 13: Education and Awareness

Raising awareness about the impacts of fashion is essential for fostering a culture of sustainability. Educational initiatives, from school programs to industry workshops, can empower individuals to make informed choices. By understanding the social and environmental consequences of their consumption, consumers can make more conscious decisions and support sustainable practices.

Schools and universities play a vital role in educating the next generation about sustainable fashion. Incorporating sustainability into fashion design and business curricula can equip students with the knowledge and skills needed to create and promote eco-friendly clothing. Initiatives like the Sustainable Fashion Academy and the Fashion Institute of Technology's Sustainable Fashion program are examples of how education can drive change in the industry.

Industry workshops and training programs can also help professionals stay informed about the latest developments in sustainable fashion. These programs can cover topics such as sustainable materials, ethical supply chains, and circular economy principles, providing valuable insights and best practices for brands and designers. By investing in education and training, the fashion industry can build a workforce that is knowledgeable and committed to sustainability.

Public awareness campaigns are another powerful tool for driving change.

Campaigns like Fashion Revolution's "Who Made My Clothes?" movement have successfully raised awareness about the ethical and environmental issues in the fashion industry, encouraging consumers to ask questions and demand greater transparency from brands. By engaging the public and sparking conversations, these campaigns can create a broader cultural shift towards sustainability.

14

Chapter 14: Future of Sustainable Fashion

The future of fashion lies in the hands of innovators and changemakers who are committed to sustainability. Emerging trends and technologies are paving the way for a more sustainable and ethical fashion industry. From digital fashion to regenerative agriculture, the possibilities are endless, and the fashion industry has the potential to lead the way in creating a more sustainable world.

Digital fashion is one of the most exciting developments in the industry. By creating virtual garments that can be worn in digital spaces, such as social media and video games, designers can reduce the need for physical clothing and the associated environmental impacts. Digital fashion allows for endless creativity and personalization, offering a new way for consumers to express their style without contributing to waste and pollution. As technology continues to advance, the potential for digital fashion to transform the industry is immense.

Regenerative agriculture is another promising trend. Unlike conventional farming methods, which often deplete soil and harm ecosystems, regenerative agriculture aims to restore and enhance the health of the land. This includes practices such as crop rotation, cover cropping, and reduced tillage, which help build soil health, increase biodiversity, and sequester carbon. By sourcing materials from regenerative farms, the fashion industry can support sustainable agriculture and reduce its environmental footprint.

Innovative materials are also driving the future of sustainable fashion. From lab-grown leather to biodegradable fabrics, new materials are offering more eco-friendly alternatives to traditional textiles. Companies like MycoWorks and Bolt Threads are developing materials made from fungi and spider silk, respectively, which have the potential to revolutionize the industry. As research and development continue to advance, the fashion industry will have access to a broader range of sustainable materials, helping to reduce its environmental impact.

15

Chapter 15: Case Studies in Sustainability

Real-world examples of sustainability in fashion can provide valuable insights and inspiration. This chapter will present case studies of brands and initiatives that have successfully implemented sustainable practices, offering lessons and best practices for others to follow. From zero-waste design to ethical supply chains, these case studies will showcase the possibilities of sustainable fashion.

Patagonia is often cited as a leader in sustainable fashion. The brand has built its reputation on environmental stewardship, with initiatives such as the Worn Wear program, which encourages customers to buy used clothing and repair their garments rather than buy new ones. Patagonia's commitment to sustainability extends to its supply chain, where the company works to ensure fair labor practices and reduce its environmental impact. By prioritizing transparency and social responsibility, Patagonia sets a high standard for the industry.

Stella McCartney is another notable example. As a pioneer of vegan fashion, McCartney has made a name for herself by refusing to use leather, fur, and other animal products in her collections. Her brand is known for its innovative use of sustainable materials, such as recycled polyester and organic cotton. McCartney's commitment to sustainability is reflected in every aspect of her business, from design to production to marketing.

Eileen Fisher is a brand that has embraced the principles of the circular economy. The company's Renew program collects and resells used Eileen Fisher garments, giving them a second life and reducing waste. Fisher also invests in sustainable materials and fair labor practices, working to create a more ethical and environmentally friendly fashion industry. By focusing on longevity and circularity, Eileen Fisher offers a model for other brands to follow.

16

Chapter 16: The Impact of COVID-19

The COVID-19 pandemic has disrupted the fashion industry, highlighting both its vulnerabilities and its potential for change. Supply chain disruptions, shifts in consumer behavior, and economic uncertainties have forced the industry to reevaluate its practices and adapt to new realities. The pandemic has also underscored the importance of sustainability and resilience in the fashion industry.

One of the most significant impacts of the pandemic has been on the supply chain. Factory closures, transportation restrictions, and labor shortages have disrupted the production and distribution of clothing. This has led to a reevaluation of supply chain practices, with many brands seeking to shorten and localize their supply chains to reduce their reliance on global networks. By sourcing materials and production locally, brands can increase their resilience and reduce their environmental footprint.

The pandemic has also accelerated the shift towards digital and e-commerce. With physical stores closed and consumers staying at home, online shopping has become the primary mode of purchasing clothing. This has opened up new opportunities for digital fashion and virtual experiences, allowing brands to engage with consumers in innovative ways. The rise of e-commerce has also highlighted the importance of sustainable packaging and shipping practices.

Consumer behavior has also changed as a result of the pandemic. Many consumers have become more conscious of their purchasing decisions, seeking out sustainable and ethical brands. The pandemic has highlighted the interconnectedness of global issues, from health and safety to environmental sustainability, leading to a greater awareness of the impact of fashion on people and the planet. This shift in consumer attitudes presents an opportunity for the fashion industry to embrace more sustainable practices and build a more resilient future.

17

Chapter 17: Sewing Change Together

The journey towards a sustainable fashion industry is a collective effort that requires collaboration and commitment from all stakeholders. This concluding chapter will emphasize the importance of working together—brands, consumers, policymakers, and activists—to create a fashion industry that respects both people and the planet. It will offer a call to action, inspiring readers to join the movement for a more sustainable and ethical future.

Brands have a crucial role to play in driving sustainability. By adopting transparent and ethical practices, investing in sustainable materials and technologies, and prioritizing fair labor practices, brands can lead the way in creating a more responsible fashion industry. Collaboration between brands, suppliers, and other stakeholders is essential to address the complex challenges of sustainability and create meaningful change.

Consumers also have a powerful voice in shaping the future of fashion. By making informed and conscious choices, supporting sustainable brands, and advocating for greater transparency and accountability, consumers can drive demand for responsible fashion. Consumer activism, through campaigns and movements, can hold brands accountable and push for industry-wide change. Every purchase is an opportunity to support a more sustainable and ethical fashion industry.

Policymakers play a critical role in creating an enabling environment for sustainability. By implementing regulations and standards that promote environmental and social responsibility, governments can drive significant improvements in the fashion industry. Policy measures, such as carbon taxes, labor protections, and incentives for sustainable practices, can create a level playing field and encourage brands to adopt more sustainable practices.

Activists and organizations also play a vital role in driving change. By raising awareness, advocating for policy changes, and holding brands accountable, they can help create a more just and sustainable fashion industry. Collaboration between activists, brands, and policymakers is essential to address the systemic issues in the fashion industry and create lasting change.

The Sustainable Stitch: How Fashion, Ecology, and Ethics Are Sewing Change

Fashion is an ever-evolving reflection of our cultural values, aspirations, and identities. Yet, beneath the allure of the latest trends lies a complex web of environmental and ethical challenges. "The Sustainable Stitch" unravels this intricate tapestry, exploring the fashion industry's impact on our world and the transformative potential of sustainable practices.

Through 17 thought-provoking chapters, this book delves into the history of fashion, from its revolutionary beginnings to the rise of fast fashion and its associated ethical concerns. It examines the environmental cost of garment production, highlighting the issues of water usage, chemical waste, and plastic pollution. With a focus on the power of consumers and the influence of sustainable style icons, the book underscores the importance of informed choices and mindful shopping.

Green innovations and the principles of the circular economy are presented as viable solutions to the fashion industry's challenges. Real-world case studies of brands like Patagonia, Stella McCartney, and Eileen Fisher offer inspiring examples of sustainability in action. The book also addresses the impact of the COVID-19 pandemic, showcasing the industry's resilience and adaptability.

"The Sustainable Stitch" serves as a call to action, urging collaboration among brands, consumers, policymakers, and activists to create a fashion industry that respects both people and the planet. With its comprehensive

CHAPTER 17: SEWING CHANGE TOGETHER

insights and practical tips, this book empowers readers to join the movement for a more sustainable and ethical future in fashion.

www.ingramcontent.com/pod-product-compliance
Lightning Source LLC
LaVergne TN
LVHW020459080526
838202LV00057B/6056